A GOOD ROUND UP COOK
LARAMIE PLAINS — E RANCH —

De Smet, South Dakota

PORK TENDERLOIN BBQ

2½   lbs. boneless pork tenderloin

MARINADE:

¼   cup honey
1   cup ketchup
1   Tbsp. liquid smoke
2   Tbsp. cayenne pepper sauce
1   tsp. onion powder
1   clove garlic, minced
1   tsp. ginger

⅛   tsp. paprika
1   Tbsp. soy sauce
1   Tbsp. white wine Worcestershire sauce
1½   Tbsp. Worcestershire sauce
1   tsp. dry mustard
•   Dash of white & black pepper

In a bowl, mix together all the marinade ingredients. Cut the tenderloin in thick strips. Place pork in a container that has a secure lid, and pour marinade over the pork to cover completely. Seal with lid and refrigerate at least 2 hours or overnight, turning pork over in the sauce several times. Grill slowly over warm coals, with the coals pushed to the side, until done.

SUN GLAZED SWEET POTATOES

2   cups cooked sweet potatoes
½   cup pure maple syrup
¼   cup butter

In a saucepan, combine maple syrup and butter. Bring to a boil and boil rapidly for 5 minutes until thickened. Pour over sweet potatoes. Bake at 350 degrees for 15 to 20 minutes.

Badlands National Park – one of many obstacles that confronted the westward bound pioneer.

WILD WEST CABBAGE SLAW

⅓	cup mayonnaise	1	small onion, chopped
⅓	cup sour cream	½	cup chopped green pepper
1	tsp. brown sugar	1	can black beans, drained
1½	tsp. dried dill	4	oz. turkey breast, cubed
•	Salt & pepper to taste	1	red apple
2	cups each shredded red and green cabbage		

*C*ream together the mayonnaise, sour cream, brown sugar, dill, salt and pepper until well blended. In a separate bowl, toss together the remaining ingredients. Drizzle the creamed sauce over the cabbage and gently toss to cover the mixture. Chill before serving. Yield: 4 servings.

FRESH TROUT WITH MUSTARD SAUCE

4	fresh trout fillets	⅓	cup red wine vinegar
8	bacon slices	¼	cup steak sauce
•	Salt & pepper to taste	1	tsp. Worcestershire sauce
½	cup mustard		

Wash trout and pat dry with paper towels. Lay bacon in a shallow baking pan and place the trout on top of bacon. Sprinkle with salt and pepper. Cover with foil, sealing the edges. Bake at 375 degrees for 20 to 25 minutes. Mix together mustard, red wine vinegar, steak sauce and Worcestershire sauce until smooth. Garnish the trout with mustard sauce, parsley and lemon wedges.

OLD FASHIONED COLE SLAW

1	head cabbage, cut thin/shredded	1	Tbsp. butter
1	pint vinegar	3	Tbsp. sugar
1	egg, beaten	•	Salt & pepper to taste

Place cut cabbage in a dish. Sprinkle with salt and pepper. Heat vinegar to scalding point, then quickly beat in egg, butter and sugar. Pour over cabbage and refrigerate.

Roughlock Falls – Fresh water, a daily necessity

SOURDOUGH STARTER

1	cup flour	1	pkg. yeast
1	cup water		

*M*ix all the ingredients together in a pint jar. Let stand in a warm place overnight to ferment.

SOURDOUGH BREAD

1	cup milk	2	Tbsp. lukewarm water
⅓	cup sugar	1½	cups sourdough starter
⅓	cup shortening	5	cups flour
1	tsp. salt		
1	pkg. active dry yeast or 1		
	cake compressed yeast		

*S*cald milk; add sugar, shortening and salt. Stir to melt sugar and shortening; cook to lukewarm. Dissolve yeast in warm water. Beat together cooled milk mixture, yeast, sourdough starter and 2 cups flour. Add remaining flour to make a stiff dough. Turn onto floured surface, knead 5 to 10 minutes. Add only enough flour to keep from sticking. Place in a greased bowl, turning to grease surface. Let rise for 1½ hours or until double in size. Punch down, let rise again for about 30 minutes. Divide into 2 balls, cover with towel and let rise for 10 minutes. Shape into 2 loaves and put each in a greased 9" x 5" x 3" pan. Let rise for about 1 hour or until double in size. Bake at 400 degrees for 30 to 40 minutes. Turn out and cool.

QUAIL PIE

6	quail, dressed	¼	cup diced green onions
¼	cup butter	½	cup diced celery
5	Tbsp. flour	½	lb. diced cooked ham
½	tsp. salt	2	cans (8 oz.) chicken broth
⅛	tsp. pepper	¼	cup water
½	lb. fresh mushrooms	•	Salt & pepper to taste

In a cast iron skillet, melt butter and sauté quail that has been coated with 3 Tbsp. flour, salt and pepper. Remove quail once it is golden brown. In remaining butter, add mushrooms, onions, and celery; sauté until tender. Add ham and chicken broth. Stir in 2 Tbsp. flour and water. Boil and let thicken, stirring constantly. Pour mixture into a 2 qt. baking dish with quail.

CRUST:		2/3	cup shortening
1	cup flour	1/2	tsp. salt

In a medium bowl, combine flour, shortening, and salt. When mixture resembles cornmeal, add a little cold milk a little at a time until it holds together in a ball. Flatten on a floured board and roll out to the shape of baking dish. Flute edges and slash vents to allow steam to escape. Bake at 350 degrees for 50 to 60 minutes.

AUNT CAROLYN'S WALDORF SALAD

1	cup apples, chopped	1	cup nuts, chopped
1	cup celery, chopped	2	cups miniature marshmallows
1	cup crushed pineapple (drained - optional)	½	cup raisins

Blend the above ingredients, mixing well. Make Lemon Sauce.

	LEMON SAUCE:	1½	Tbsp. flour
•	Juice of ½ lemon	•	Small amount of water
1	cup sugar	½	cup sweet cream

Combine ingredients in a saucepan. Use a small amount of water, as you will want to make a thick sauce. When thickened, remove from heat and cool. Add sweet cream to sauce and pour over other ingredients, mixing thoroughly. The lemon sauce makes the difference, also keeps the apples white. Try adding grapes – great.

WESTERN ONION SOUP

1	qt. beef stock or 2 cans beef broth, double strength	2	cups thinly sliced onions
4	tsp. Worcestershire sauce	4	French Bread slices
1	stick butter	4	Swiss cheese slices
		•	Butter for bread slices

Melt butter in a saucepan. Add onions and sauté for about 5 minutes, stirring often. Add beef stock and Worcestershire sauce. Simmer for 20 minutes. Lightly butter bread slices and toast them. Place a slice of toasted bread in bottom of each soup bowl. Ladle soup into bowls. Top with a slice of Swiss cheese. Heat under the broiler flame to melt cheese. May place in the microwave until cheese melts.

CHEESY GREEN TOMATO PIE

1	9" pie shell	3	Tbsp. butter
1	pkg. (8 oz.) Cheddar cheese, shredded	6	medium green tomatoes, cut in chunks
1	large onion, chopped	2	Tbsp. flour
1	small green bell pepper, chopped	•	Salt and pepper to taste
1	clove garlic	•	Parsley flakes

*D*ivide shredded Cheddar cheese evenly. Sprinkle half of the cheese in the bottom of the pie shell and set aside. Sauté onions, green pepper, and garlic in the butter for 3 to 5 minutes. Add chopped green tomatoes and cook over medium-high heat for 15 minutes. Add flour and stir until blended. Add salt and pepper to taste. Pour tomato mixture into the pie shell and sprinkle remaining cheese over the top of the pie. Evenly dash parsley flakes over the pie and bake at 400 degrees for about 10-12 minutes or until brown and bubbly.

SKILLET BROWNED SPUDS

6	large potatoes, cubed	1	bouillon cube, beef or chicken
1	onion, chopped	1	Tbsp. Italian seasoning
¼	cup chopped green pepper	2	Tbsp. bacon bits
¾	stick butter	•	Pepper and paprika
¼	cup water		

*W*ash potatoes, leave skins on, and cube. Place potatoes in a skillet and add onions and green peppers. In a saucepan, melt butter, add water and bouillon cube. Heat on low to dissolve the bouillon cube completely. Add Italian seasoning to melted butter mixture. Stir well and drizzle over the potatoes. Sprinkle potatoes with bacon bits, pepper and paprika. Fry in the skillet for about 35 minutes or until nicely browned. Turn potatoes with a spatula occasionally to prevent sticking. Add more butter if needed.

Native Americans were a common sight along the trail.

BUFFALO STEAK

- 4-5 lbs. buffalo loin steaks (or beef steaks)
- Salt & pepper

MARINADE:

2	cups dry red wine	½	tsp. thyme
½	cup vinegar	3	cloves garlic, pressed
2	Tbsp. lemon juice	2	tsp. Worcestershire sauce
2	small bay leaves	1	onion, diced
2	Tbsp. parsley flakes	3	Tbsp. butter

In a saucepan, combine the marinade ingredients and cook on low heat for 5 minutes. Let cool. Rub the buffalo steaks with salt and pepper. Pour marinade over the steaks and refrigerate for at least 8 hours or overnight. Remove meat and cook over hot coals until done, basting as it cooks.

ROASTED PHEASANT

3	pheasants	2	large potatoes, cubed
•	Salt & pepper	1½	shallots, chopped
3	carrots	1	clove garlic
2	stalks celery	2	small bay leaves
2	onions, sliced in rings		
1	green pepper or banana pepper strips		

Rub pheasants with salt and pepper. Preheat oven to 450 degrees and brown pheasants until golden in color. Place the pheasants in a large stockpot with the remaining ingredients. Cover with water and simmer for about 2 hours, or until done.

Evidence of the westward journey still apparent in this picture of the Oregon Trail.

TUMBLEWEED CAKE

1	cup quick-cooking oats	1½	tsp. cinnamon
1½	cups boiling water	½	tsp. nutmeg
1	cup brown sugar, packed	1½	Tbsp. cocoa
1	cup sugar	1½	cups flour
½	cup butter	½	tsp. salt
2	eggs, beaten	1½	tsp. baking powder
2	Tbsp. molasses	1	pkg. semi-sweet chocolate chips
1	cup chopped walnuts or pecans		

*P*our boiling water over the quick oats and set aside. In a separate bowl, cream together brown sugar, sugar, butter, eggs, and molasses. Stir this mixture into the quick oats and add walnuts or pecans. In a separate bowl, combine cinnamon, nutmeg, cocoa, flour, salt, and baking powder. Mix all of the dry ingredients together. Gradually add the dry ingredients to the oats mixture and add chocolate chips; beat together well. Pour batter into a greased cake pan. Bake at 350 degrees for 40 minutes or until toothpick inserted comes out clean. Frost with Butter Cream Frosting.

BUTTER CREAM FROSTING

1	cup butter flavored shortening	½	cup evaporated milk
2	boxes powdered sugar	½	tsp. vanilla
1	pkg. (8oz.) cream cheese		

*B*eat together shortening and powdered sugar. Add cream cheese and milk and beat well for 5 minutes. Add vanilla and beat an additional 5 minutes until smooth and creamy.

COWBOY POTATO CAKES

6	medium potatoes	1½	Tbsp. chopped parsley
3	Tbsp. butter	½	onion, chopped
2	eggs	1	cup ham, cubed
¼	cup mayonnaise	1	pkg. (8 oz.) shredded cheese
•	Salt & pepper to taste	1	cup flour or more if needed

*W*ash potatoes, leaving the skins on. Cut in quarters and boil in salted water until tender. Mash potatoes with butter, eggs, mayonnaise, salt and pepper, and parsley. Mix well. Add onions, ham, cheese and flour. Mix well for a sticky dough. Form into patties and sprinkle with flour on both sides. Fry in hot oil for about 10 minutes on each side or until golden brown on both sides.

SUNRISE MUFFINS

¼	cup butter	2	tsp. baking powder
1	egg	½	tsp. salt
⅓	cup sugar	½	cup milk
1½	cups flour	¾	cup crisp bacon pieces

*I*n a bowl, cream together butter, egg and sugar until well beaten. Add the flour, baking powder and salt. Slowly add milk and mix until blended. Stir in bacon pieces and spoon into 12 greased muffin tins. Bake at 400 degrees for 15 to 20 minutes or until golden brown on top.

Spearfish Canyon – Beautiful yet treacherous vistas often caused major traveling problems.

HOE CAKE WITH DUTCH HONEY

2½	cups self rising flour	1	cup milk
4	Tbsp. oil		

Mix flour and milk together. Warm oil in an iron skillet and pour warm oil into flour mixture; mix well to make a sticky dough. Put dough on a floured surface and knead a couple of times. Shape dough in a circle and place in skillet on top of the stove. Cook on low heat for 15 minutes and then turn over and cook for 15 minutes more. Turn onto a plate and serve with butter, syrup and Dutch Honey.

DUTCH HONEY:

1	cup sugar	1	cup dark syrup
1	cup sour cream	1	tsp. vanilla

Cook sugar, sour cream and syrup until creamy; stir often. Remove from heat and add vanilla. Store in refrigerator. Serve over hoe cake, pancakes or bread.

OZ & TTA WAGONS

SUNDANCE PUDDING

1	egg, beaten	•	Dash of salt
¾	cup sugar	1	cup chopped apple
2	Tbsp. flour	½	cup pecans
1¼	tsp. baking powder		

*B*eat sugar and egg until creamy. Sift flour, baking powder and salt into egg mixture. Mix well. Add apple and pecans; mix well. Pour into a buttered 8" pie plate. Bake at 350 degrees for 35 minutes or until golden brown. Do not be dismayed when this pudding rises high, then falls before time to remove it from the oven. Serve plain or with whipped cream or vanilla ice cream. Serve hot, warm or cold. Yield: 4 to 5 servings.

FRONTIER BREAD

8	cups flour	¼	cup sugar
½	cup warm water	1	Tbsp. salt
3	pkgs. dry yeast	2½	cups warm water

*D*issolve yeast in 1/2 cup warm water. Stir in sugar until dissolved and let stand 10-15 minutes, until mixture becomes bubbly. In a large bowl, combine the flour to the sugar and yeast mixture, gradually adding the warm water until the dough becomes stiff. Transfer dough to a greased bowl and allow it to rise in a warm place to double in size. Puncture the dough and form into loaves and place in greased loaf pans. Cover with a towel and let rise again to double in size. Bake at 350 degrees for one hour, until tops of loaves are golden brown.

STAMPEDE STEW

2½	lbs. beef, cubed		1	green pepper, cut in strips
2½	Tbsp. flour		1	clove garlic
1	Tbsp. paprika		1	can tomatoes & green chilies
1	tsp. chili powder		1	tsp. ground cloves
⅛	tsp. black pepper		2	cups each, chopped carrots
3	Tbsp. butter			& potatoes
2	onions, sliced		2	stalks celery, chopped

*M*ix together flour, paprika, chili powder, and black pepper. Roll cubed beef in flour mixture and brown in a skillet with butter. In a large stockpot add browned beef and the remaining ingredients except carrots, potatoes and celery. Simmer for 2 hours. Then add the vegetables and simmer an additional 45 minutes or until vegetables are tender. Add water as needed. Yield: 6-8 servings.

ELK SIRLOIN STEAKS

4 Elk sirloin steaks

MARINADE:

¼	cup pineapple juice	2	Tbsp. soy sauce
½	cup salad oil	¼	cup chili sauce
¼	cup honey	•	Salt & pepper

Combine pineapple juice, oil, honey, soy sauce and chili sauce. Season steaks with salt and pepper. Pour marinade over the steaks and let stand for at least 2 hours in the refrigerator, turn steaks in the sauce to coat well. Cook steaks over hot coals until done.

CHUCKWAGON BAKED BEANS

1	lb. navy beans	¼	cup molasses
¼	lb. salt pork, diced	1	Tbsp. dry mustard
1	cup chopped onion	¼	tsp. black pepper
¼	cup green pepper	1	Tbsp. Worcestershire sauce
1	cup ketchup	1	tsp. liquid smoke
¼	cup dark brown sugar		

Place beans in a covered iron kettle, add enough water to completely cover the beans and let soak overnight. Drain and add 1 qt. cold water. Bring to a boil, cut the heat down and simmer for 2 hours. In a skillet lightly brown the salt pork, onions and peppers. Remove and add this to the iron kettle with the beans and the remaining ingredients. Cover and cook over low heat for about 6 hours. Stir occasionally and do not let the beans dry out, add water if necessary during the cooking process.

CORN SALAD RELISH

2	ears corn cut from cob	½	cup sugar
½	head cabbage, chopped	2	Tbsp. mustard
1	bunch celery, chopped	1	Tbsp. salt, or to taste
1	large onion, chopped	2	cups vinegar
½	cup diced sweet red pepper		

Mix and boil all ingredients for 30 minutes. Set aside, allow to cool and refrigerate.

1880 Train – Black Hills, South Dakota

Steamboat Rock – Bighorn Mountain Range, Wyoming

FRIED CHICKEN

1	fryer, cut up	1	tsp. red pepper
½	cup flour	•	Salt & pepper
½	cup bread crumbs		

Wash chicken; season with salt and pepper. Mix together flour, bread crumbs, and red pepper; dredge chicken in flour mixture. Fry in hot oil until golden brown on both sides. Drain on brown paper.

PRAIRIE CARROTS

2	cups carrots, sliced lengthwise	½	cup mayonnaise
¼	cup liquid from carrots	•	Salt & pepper to taste
2	Tbsp. grated onion	1¼	cup bread crumbs
1	Tbsp. horseradish	•	Butter
1	Tbsp. mustard	•	Paprika

Cook carrots and reserve 1/4 cup of the liquid from the carrots. Place carrots in a baking dish. Mix together liquid from carrots, grated onion, horseradish, mustard, mayonnaise, salt and pepper. Pour mixture over carrots. Top with bread crumbs. Add dollops of butter and sprinkle with paprika. Bake at 375 degrees for 15 to 20 minutes.

FRESH BEANS & NEW POTATOES

1½	lb. green beans, snapped	2	Tbsp. oil
4	new potatoes, quartered	1	onion, chopped
1	small ham bone	1½	cups minced ham
•	Water	•	Salt & pepper to taste

Wash and snap green beans into a big kettle. Wash and quarter new potatoes, may add more potatoes if desired, and place in the kettle. Add ham bone and enough water to cover completely. Add remaining ingredients and simmer for at least 2½ hours or until green beans and potatoes are soft. Add water as needed. Remove ham bone and serve.

SWEET HONEY BREAD

6	cups flour	5	Tbsp. honey
1	Tbsp. salt·	2	cups warm water
5	Tbsp. butter or margarine, melted	2	pkgs. active dry yeast
		3	eggs

*D*issolve yeast in water and set aside. In a large mixing bowl, combine 2 cups flour, salt, butter and honey. Gradually add yeast and water mixture. Beat together well. Add eggs; beat well for about 2 minutes. Stir in remaining flour to make a soft dough. Cover and place in a warm place until dough doubles in size, about 45 minutes. Punch down dough and turn out onto a lightly floured board. Divide into 2 balls. Shape each ball into a loaf. Place in two greased 9" x 5" x 3" loaf pans. Cover and let rise again until double in size. Bake at 375 degrees for 35 to 40 minutes. Let cool and remove from pans to a wire rack to prevent "sweating."

SOUR CREAM COFFEE CAKE

2	eggs	1¼	cups flour
¾	cup sour cream	½	tsp. baking soda
1	cup sugar	1	tsp. baking powder
1	tsp. vanilla	•	Pinch of salt

Beat eggs and sour cream together until well mixed. Add sugar and beat for 1 minute. Add vanilla and mix well. Sift flour, baking soda, baking powder and salt into the egg mixture. Stir in thoroughly. Pour batter into a greased 9-inch cake pan. Dot with butter and sprinkle with sugar and cinnamon to taste. Bake at 350 degrees for 25 to 30 minutes or until toothpick inserted in center comes out clean.

BOUNTY BERRY PIE

4	cups blackberries/black raspberries, or your favorite berries	3	Tbsp. cornstarch
		⅛	tsp. nutmeg
		¼	tsp. vanilla
2	cups sugar	1	pkg. prepared pie crust
⅔	cup flour		

Combine berries, sugar, flour, cornstarch, nutmeg and vanilla in a bowl. Mix well and pour into the prepared pie crust. Cut second pie crust into strips and form a lattice top on pie. Bake at 375 degrees for 50 minutes or until done.

Pioneer travel

CORNMEAL ROLLS

1½	cups flour	¼	tsp. baking soda
¾	cup coarse cornmeal	¼	cup vegetable shortening
4	tsp. baking powder	1	egg
1	tsp. salt	¾	cup buttermilk

Sift together the dry ingredients. Cut in shortening. Beat the egg slightly with the milk and add to the dry ingredients. Toss on a floured surface, knead slightly. Roll to ½" thickness and cut with a large biscuit cutter. With the back of a knife, make a crease just off center on each round. Brush with butter and fold the smaller part over. Press the fold gently. Bake at 450 degrees for 12 to 15 minutes. Serve hot.

SKILLET FRIED CATFISH

4	fresh catfish	½	tsp. paprika
1	cup flour	•	Salt & pepper
¼	cup cornmeal	•	Oil & butter

Season flour with salt, pepper and paprika. Wash fresh catfish and dredge in flour mixture. Pan fry in hot oil and add about 2 Tbsp. butter to oil. Fry until golden brown on both sides.

BAKED CABBAGE

1	head white cabbage	1	cup grated cheese
3	Tbsp. butter	•	Salt & pepper to taste
1	Tbsp. flour	8	crackers, crushed
1	cup water	½	red pepper, chopped
1	large yellow onion		

Boil cabbage for 15 minutes in salted water. Drain and add more water, bring to a boil and let simmer until tender. Drain, reserve 1 cup of stock from cabbage and set the cabbage aside to cool. Melt butter in a saucepan and stir in flour. Add stock, water, onions and season with salt and pepper. Let cook on low heat to blend, stirring occasionally. Once all is warm, add cheese, let cook until the cheese melts. Chop cabbage in strips and place in a greased baking dish. Pour sauce over the cabbage and sprinkle crushed crackers and chopped red peppers over the top. Bake at 425 degrees for 10 minutes or until heated through.

BLACK KETTLE CHILI

1	lb. pinto beans	1	can black beans
3	medium onions, chopped	2	cans tomato sauce
1	clove garlic, minced	½	Tbsp. crushed red peppers
½	cup zucchini, chopped	1	pkg. chili seasoning
¼	cup green pepper, chopped	•	Salt & pepper to taste
1	can tomatoes & green chilies	3	Tbsp. chili powder
1	lb. ground venison	1	Tbsp. ground cumin

*P*lace pinto beans in a bowl, add enough water to cover the beans, let soak overnight. Drain and reserve 1 cup of the liquid. Lightly brown ground venison in a little butter. In a heavy dutch oven add beans, ground venison and remaining ingredients. Simmer over low heat for about 8 hours or until done. Stir occasionally, add water if needed as it cooks.

CORN BREAD

1½	cups yellow cornmeal	2	Tbsp. butter
1½	cups milk	2½	tsp. baking powder
1	tsp. salt	1	egg, separated

*S*immer milk until tiny bubbles form around the edge, but do not boil. Add cornmeal and stir in salt and butter. Beat egg yolk and baking powder, add to mixture, stir really well. Grease an 8" x 8" pan and heat in oven. Remove and immediately pour batter into the hot pan. This makes a good crust. Bake in a preheated 400 degree oven for 20 minutes. Serve hot, cut in squares.

Devils Tower – First National Monument

JALAPEÑO CHEESE SQUARES

1	lb. mild Cheddar cheese, shredded	1	jar (12-oz.) sliced jalapeños, drained
1	lb. Monterey Jack cheese, shredded	1	can evaporated milk
1	cup sharp Cheddar cheese, shredded	1	cup flour
		2	eggs, beaten

Combine the three cheeses together in a large mixing bowl. Place 1/2 of the cheese into a 13" X 9" X 2" baking dish. Layer sliced jalapeños over cheese and then top with remaining cheese. Beat eggs, milk and flour together until smooth. Pour mixture over cheese and jalapeños. Bake at 325 degrees for 60 to 70 minutes, until lightly brown. Remove from oven and let cool completely. Cut into 1" squares. Yield: 10 - 20 servings.

CHICKEN & DUMPLINGS

1	stewing chicken (4-6 lbs.), cut in pieces	1	onion, chopped
2	stalks celery, chopped	4	peppercorns
2	carrots, chopped	1	clove garlic, minced
		•	Salt & black pepper to taste

DUMPLINGS:

2	cups flour	¾	cup milk
3	tsp. baking powder	1	Tbsp. chopped parsley
1	tsp. salt	•	Black pepper to taste
1½	Tbsp. butter	1	egg, beaten

Place chicken in a large pot and cover with water. Add celery, carrots, onions, peppercorns, garlic, salt and pepper to taste. Simmer for 1-1/2 to 2 hours or until chicken is tender. Remove chicken and vegetables. In a bowl, combine flour, baking powder, salt and cut in butter with a fork or pastry blender. Beat milk and egg together. Stir into dry ingredients until all is moistened, should be thick enough to drop from a spoon. Place batter on a plate and drop into boiling broth by spoonfuls. Cover pan and simmer for 12 to 15 minutes. Place chicken and dumplings on a platter with broth spooned over them. Garnish with chopped parsley.

SOURDOUGH BISCUITS

2	cups flour	¾	tsp. salt
1	Tbsp. sugar	2	cups sourdough starter
1	Tbsp. baking powder	2-3	Tbsp. softened lard or butter

Sift flour, sugar, baking powder and salt into a large bowl; pour in starter. (See page 5 for starter recipe.) Mix to make a firm dough. Grease a 12" iron skillet with lard. Pinch off balls the size of walnuts. Place in a skillet. Set biscuits in a warm place for 10 to 15 minutes. Bake at 400 degrees in skillet for 24-30 minutes.

SETTLERS CORN CHOWDER

6	slices bacon	1	cup cream
2	cans corn, drained	2	cups sharp Cheddar cheese
1½	cups onion, chopped	1	tsp. thyme, crushed
1½	cups celery, chopped	1	Tbsp. Worcestershire sauce
4	medium potatoes, diced	2	Tbsp. fresh parsley, minced
1	cup chicken broth	•	Salt & pepper to taste
3	cups milk		

Fry bacon in a skillet until crisp. Remove bacon and reserve bacon drippings. Sauté onion and celery in reserved bacon drippings until transparent and tender. Add potatoes and chicken broth and simmer for about 20 minutes or until potatoes are tender. Add the remaining ingredients. Cook over medium heat, stirring constantly until corn is hot and cheese is melted, being careful not to boil. Salt and pepper to taste. Garnish with crumbles of bacon. Yield: 6 servings.

Wild Flowers, Balsam Root – Grand Teton National Park.

It was the leadership of these great Presidents that pioneered our great nation.

COW POKE BBQ RIBS

3-4	lbs. beef ribs	⅔	cup brown sugar
•	Salt & pepper	2	Tbsp. Worcestershire sauce
1	small onion, chopped	1	can tomato sauce
1½	tsp. butter	3	Tbsp. dry mustard
1	bottle chili sauce	1	tsp. black pepper

Salt and pepper the ribs on both sides. Sauté onion in butter until tender. Mix together remainder of the ingredients and add onion. Simmer for 15 minutes and then brush on ribs. Cook over warm coals, basting with sauce until done.

WAGON WHEEL SAUCE

2	medium onions, chopped	2½	Tbsp. dry mustard
1	bottle chili sauce	1	cup strong coffee
⅔	cup brown sugar	2	tsp. chili powder
2	Tbsp. Worcestershire sauce	3	cloves garlic, minced
1	bottle ketchup	•	Salt & black pepper to taste

Sauté onions in butter until tender. Mix together remainder of the ingredients and add onions. Simmer for 15 minutes.

BBQ BRISKET

5-7	lbs. beef brisket, fat removed	¼	cup lemon juice
•	Meat tenderizer	1½	Tbsp. celery seed
1½	cups chili sauce	2	cups warm beer
½	cup ketchup	1	tsp. black pepper
1½	Tbsp. chili powder	2	tsp. salt
3	Tbsp. liquid smoke	1	tsp. ground cayenne pepper
½	cup Worcestershire sauce		

Sprinkle meat tenderizer on both sides of the brisket. Place brisket in a large baking dish. Mix together the remaining ingredients and pour over the brisket. Bake at 325 degrees for 3½ to 4 hours or until meat is tender. Baste brisket often during the cooking time.

29

FARMER'S APPLE FRITTERS

2	cups flour	1	tsp. brown sugar
1	Tbsp. baking powder	2	eggs, beaten
½	tsp. salt	1	cup milk
3	Tbsp. sugar	2	cups tart apples, chopped
1	tsp. cinnamon	•	Powdered sugar

Combine flour, baking powder, salt, sugar, and cinnamon together. In a separate bowl, beat eggs and milk together. Combine milk mixture gradually to the flour mixture. Add apples and refrigerate for 1 hour. Drop by spoonfuls into hot oil and cook for 5 minutes or until golden brown on all sides. Remove from oil and roll in powdered sugar.

NANNY'S SUGAR COOKIES

1	cup butter	2	Tbsp. heavy cream
2	cups sugar	2	cups flour
2	eggs	2	tsp. baking powder
2	tsp. vanilla extract	½	tsp. cream of tartar

Cream butter and sugar until fluffy. Add eggs, vanilla and cream; mix well. Sift the flour with the baking powder and cream of tartar twice and add to the batter, mixing well. Chill thoroughly. On a well-floured surface, with a floured rolling pin, roll out small amounts of the dough to ⅛" thickness, keeping the rest of the dough chilled. Cut cookies with a 2½" cutter and place on greased cookie sheets. Sprinkle with sugar. Bake at 375 degrees for 10 to 12 minutes or until browned and crisp.

PUMPKIN PIE

2	eggs, well beaten	¼	tsp. ginger
⅔	cup sugar	¼	tsp. salt
1	cup pumpkin	½	cup whole milk
¼	tsp. cinnamon	1	pie crust, unbaked
¼	tsp. nutmeg		

Mix all ingredients well and pour into unbaked pie crust and sprinkle top with cinnamon. Bake 20 minutes at 425 degrees, reduce heat to 325 and continue baking for 20 minutes. Let cool before serving and top with whipped cream.

PRAIRIE CHICKEN SALAD

- Whole chicken
- Celery
- Mayonnaise dressing
- Hard-boiled eggs

*B*oil the chicken until tender; remove all the fat, gristle, and skin; mince the meat in small pieces. To one chicken, put 2½ times its weight in celery, cut in pieces of about one-quarter of an inch; mix thoroughly and set it in a cool place. Prepare the mayonnaise dressing, and when ready to serve, pour dressing over the chicken and celery, tossing and mixing it thoroughly. Garnish with celery tips, cold hard-boiled eggs, lettuce leaves from the heart, cold boiled beets, capers or olives. Crisp cabbage is a good substitute for celery; when celery is not used, use celery vinegar in the dressing. Turkey also makes a fine salad.

MAYONNAISE DRESSING:

2	egg yolks	½	tsp. paprika
¼	cup vinegar	1	pint (2 cups) salad oil
½	tsp. dry mustard	1	tsp. salt

*B*eat egg yolks and add a few drops of vinegar. Drop oil, drop by drop, into egg mixture until 1/4 cup is used (beating all the time). Then gradually increase amount of oil added, beating constantly. As mixture thickens, add rest of vinegar a little at a time. Add salt, mustard and paprika. Be sure to follow the directions.